GLIMPSES OF ANNE OF CLEVES

BORN 1515—DIED 1557

A TAPESTRY, BASED ON HISTORICAL FACTS, OF THE LIFE AND TIMES OF ANNE OF CLEVES

SHUMA CHAKRAVARTY

ISBN: 978-0-9858282-3-3

Published by:
CONVERPAGE
23 Acorn Street
Scituate, MA 02066
www.converpage.com
781-378-1996

For my mother,

Uma Devi Chakravarty
and
The Five College Women's Studies Research Center

ACKNOWLEDGEMENTS

I wish to thank Pamela McCallum for her helpfulness in getting this book published.

I want to thank Craig Smith for his excellent technical expertise and editorial assistance. I designed the front cover and the back page of this book with technical assistance from Craig Smith. The front page has Hans Holbein's miniature picture of Anne of Cleves, which is in the Victoria and Albert Museum in London, England. The back page has, from left to right, a portrait of Anne of Cleves, by Hans Holbein, which is in the Louvre in Paris, France. The middle portrait is by Hiroshi Sugimoto, 1999. The portrait on the right is by Barthel Bruyn the Elder. This portrait is in St. John's College, Oxford, England. On the top of the back page is the badge of Anne of Cleves which is in the Weidenfeld and Nicholson Archive. On the front cover and the back page are two versions of the Tudor rose.

I wish to thank the Rev. Elizabeth Wheatley Dyson for writing the foreword of this book in November, 2012.

I wish to thank Professor John Burt for writing the preface of this book in November, 2012.

I wish to thank Margaret Studier, the Managing Editor of the Harvard Theological Review for her generous friendship and moral support over many years.

I wish to thank Laura Whitney, Librarian of the Harvard Divinity School Library, for her gracious interest in my scholarly work.

I wish to thank Professor Elie Wiesel for his generous appreciation of my life and work ever since I became one of his students in 1978. In a letter of recommendation that he wrote on my behalf on June 14, 2012, Elie Wiesel stated:"Sensitive and eloquent, Shuma's written work is also impressive. It shows evidence of a full command of scholarly skills."

In Memoriam

I knew Mother Teresa (b. 1910 -- d.1997) for many years and was fortunate to be loved by her. I know that Mother Teresa, who frequently asked me to "do small things with great love" and to "do something beautiful for God", would have approved of Anne of Cleves' life of chastity, generosity to the poor, unselfish kindness and hospitality to everyone, of every station, who entered her life, no matter for what duration. Yes, Anne of Cleves did many "small things with great love" on a daily basis. Towards the end of Anne of Cleves' life, she found solace in the Catholic religion of her mother, Maria of Julich, after bravely enduring for many years the religious and political upheavals of Tudor England.

Finally, I wish to state that the life of Anne of Cleves has been a source of inspiration to me.

This is a photograph of Mother Teresa and Shuma Chakravarty in Kolkata, India in 1996

Dear Shuma

The fruit of SILENCE is Prayer
The fruit of PRAYER is Faith
The fruit of FAITH is Love
The fruit of LOVE is Service
The Fruit of SERVICE is Peace

Mother Teresa

God Bless you
lee Teresa mc

DEDICATION

I wish to dedicate this book to my saintly mother Uma Devi Chakravarty and to The Five College Women's Studies Research Center located in Mt. Holyoke College in South Hadley, MA. The five colleges which comprise The Five College Women's Studies Research Center are the University of Massachusetts at Amherst, Amherst College, Hampshire College, Mount Holyoke College, and Smith College.

I was among a small number of female scholars, chosen from around the world, to be an Associate in this Center in 1997-98. It is a haven for scholars. I appreciate the cordiality that I received from both the Director of this Center, Karen Remmler and the Assistant Director, Elizabeth Lehman when I contacted them recently.
I am pleased to include the following comments from Karen Remmler, written on November 6, 2012, regarding my book on Anne of Cleves.

"On behalf of The Five College Women's Studies Research Center I am delighted to recommend Shuma Chakravarty's novel *Glimpses of Anne of Cleves* (b.1515-d.1557). Delving into the power struggles of Tudor England through the formidable acts of independence and self-preservation displayed by Anne of Cleves, this novel remembers the courage, political savvy and determination of a woman among many memorable female figures who are usually overshadowed by tragic versions of them reiterated time and again in historic documentation."

Karen Remmler, Director of The Five College Women's Studies Research Center.

FOREWORD

Nearly everyone knows that King Henry the VIII had six wives but most of us remember the infamous Anne Boleyn who was beheaded. As a long time member of the Episcopal Church which was born from the Church of England tradition, I have always been intrigued by King Henry's wives, but sadly have not done much research into Anne of Cleves. Shuma Chakravarty has given us a wonderful look into the life of Anne of Cleves as she prepares herself to become King Henry the VIII's fourth wife. If you assume that Anne of Cleves is a bride to be pitied, dear Reader, you are in for a surprise!

Written as a journal, Shuma Chakravarty paints a unique picture of Anne of Cleves from several different viewpoints. She offers us a distinctive picture of Anne of Cleves, the King's "Beloved Sister." Read on and come to know and enjoy this wife of King Henry the VIII who lived to see his daughter Mary become queen.

The Rev. Elizabeth Wheatley Dyson
Rector of
St. Andrew's Episcopal Church
17 Church St.
Hanover, MA 02339

AUTHOR'S NOTES,

Shuma Chakravarty is a scholar, writer, and published author. She has graduate degrees in English Literature (from Simmons College) and Theology from Boston University and Harvard University.

PREFACE

In Tudor England the only place more dangerous than Henry the Eighth's court was his bedchamber. Advisors rose and fell, either as they politically cut each other's throats or as they fell afoul of the King's impatience. Cardinal Wolsey, after long serving his King better than he did his God, was nevertheless accused by Henry of treason for failing to secure the annulment of the King's marriage to Catherine of Aragon, but cheated the reaper by dying as he made his way to London to defend himself. Or perhaps these advisors paid the price for standing up to Henry's desires and selfish attachment to his own whims, as did Sir Thomas More, who chose to climb the scaffold rather than march in the King's procession.

Of Henry's wives, only clever, literate, strong-willed Catherine Parr seems to have prospered, and even she only escaped arrest and execution by quick thinking. Catherine of Aragon's humiliation and rejection convulsed the politics and religious history of England for a generation. Anne Boleyn learned in the hardest way the fickleness of Henry's favor, who transformed the English church to make possible his marriage, and had her beheaded for failing to produce a son a mere three years later. Catherine Howard, beheaded for adultery after only two years of marriage to Henry, appears in history mostly as a tragic footnote. Jane Seymour died in childbirth still fully in possession of the King's love, but perhaps she was merely lucky to have died very young.

Of all Henry's wives, Anne of Cleves was perhaps the luckiest of all; never having really won the King's favor, he annulled his marriage with her early on, but afforded her a comfortable and respectable life. She comes down to us with a stigmatized reputation, since she is traditionally taken to be coarse and unattractive (but doesn't appear to be so in Holbein's famous portrait of her) and, most humiliating of all, she is remembered for her poor hygiene and powerful body odor. If that story is true, then perhaps nobody has ever owed so much to a bad smell.

Shuma Chakravarty's shrewd, insightful, and witty, brief novel *Glimpses of Anne of Cleves* offers a surprising and fascinating take about this neglected character. For one thing, Chakravarty allows Holbein himself to describe the woman he depicted, seeing her as beautiful, regal, intelligent, and charming.

Perhaps not fluent in English at the time of her marriage, and perhaps relative to Catherine Parr, a touch provincial, Anne nevertheless seems to have had the decency, good sense, and presence of mind to remain on good terms not only with her former husband who always referred to her as his " beloved sister " but also with his warring daughters, Mary and Elizabeth. Chakravarty carefully builds on these hints from the historic accounts of Anne's life to show her as keenly insightful of human nature. particularly into the complex personality of Henry, and as a generous and kind advisor to both Mary and Elizabeth. In the gilded, poisonous world of the Tudor court, Anne appears, in Chakravarty's account, to be not only able to keep her head (quite literally) but also to keep her integrity, an especially difficult feat in that time and place.

Particularly impressive is Chakravarty's treatment of Anne's political intelligence. The idea for annulment came from Anne, who is moved not only by her own physical revulsion from Henry, but also by her clear-sighted recognition that the political necessities that made her marriage valuable to Henry, no longer held, and that this marriage to her would be a political liability if he were to seek rapprochement with the Catholic powers on the European mainland. It is Anne, in Chakravarty's novel, who comes up with the annulment, as a way of enabling Henry to seek advantage in the Catholic world without offending the Protestant princes of Germany, including her own family. Anne here, and throughout the novel, is a perceptive reader of the political situation, and an insightful student of human nature.

One especially wonderful touch concerns the matter of bad smells. Here again the idea of spreading the story about Anne's body odor originates with Anne herself, as a way of justifying the annulment. But, of course, what Anne is really thinking about is the other famous "stink" in the Tudor Court, the perpetual smell of the never-healing, always festering abscess on King Henry's thigh. So rancid was that wound that one wonders whether, had Anne really had a bad smell, the King could even have scented it, masked as it would have been by the aroma of his own infection. Anne's hitting on this idea as a pretext for annulling the marriage is a such a delicious inspiration on Chakravarty's part that it made this reader clap his hands with pleasure at the brilliance of this idea.

More striking even than the shrewdness of how *Glimpses of Anne of Cleves* revises, or rather re-sees history, is its sense of its main character's decency and levelheadedness. Those were qualities in short supply in Reformation England, and are in equally short supply now.

Dr. John Burt is a Professor of English Literature at Brandeis University in Waltham, MA.

INTRODUCTION

I have been a keen student of sixteenth century England for the last ten years. Until recently, Anne of Cleves seemed a minor figure to me. However, the intensive and extensive research I have undertaken on the life of Anne of Cleves has culminated in this book. I have tried to capture the voices of Anne of Cleves, Holbein, Lowe and Hall in this work, written, as if these facts were excerpts from their diaries, to make this historical chronicle "come alive."

Extensive bibliographies of sixteenth century England are readily available. For example, Alison Weir's *Henry VIII, the King and his Court*, published in 2001, is a commendable book with an extensive bibliography. Moreover, the first major biography of Anne of Cleves, (which is *Anne of Cleves* by Elizabeth Norton) was published in 2009 and has an extensive bibliography as well. I have not included a bibliography in this book but I do include some *Primary Sources*. For those interested in further study of Tudor England, the *Letters and Papers of Henry VIII* are an extensive resource as are the writings of Edward Hall. The Spanish Imperial ambassador, Eustace Chapuys has left for posterity detailed descriptions of Anne of Cleves' arrival in England in late December, 1539 and her wedding to King Henry as well as Anne of Cleves' letter to her royal husband.

King Henry VIII (b.1491 -- d. 1547) and Anne of Cleves (b. 1515 -- d. 1557) were briefly married in 1540 because England wanted a German Protestant alliance as a buffer against the Franco-Spanish Catholic coalition which was backed by Pope Paul III who had excommunicated King Henry VIII. When the balance of power shifted quickly in Europe and France made friendly overtures towards England in 1539, there was no political necessity for the Cleves marriage.

What is fascinating, however, is King Henry VIII's adoption of Anne of Cleves (after the marriage was annulled on July 9, 1540) as his "beloved sister Anna" and his unfailing financial generosity and fraternal affection for her until the end of his life.

There is no surviving contemporary evidence that King Henry VIII ever referred to Anne of Cleves as "the Flanders Mare." This story was first written by Bishop Burnet in the seventeenth century and he gives no source for it.

I do hope that the readers of this book will be inspired by reading about the wit and wisdom, charity and clarity, goodness and generosity of Anne of Cleves.

Shuma Chakravarty
Cohasset, MA 02025.
November, 2012.

POSTSCRIPT

The following tribute to the memory of Anne of Cleves came from Simon Renard, the Spanish Imperial ambassador to England, shortly after her death in 1557. He wrote:" Everybody has nothing but good to say of Anne of Cleves."
Holinshed's Chronicles, Vol. IV : 88 praises Anne of Cleves : "A lady of right commendable regards, courteous, gentle, a good housekeeper and very bountiful to her servants."
In addition to these commendations from Anne's contemporaries, her recent English biographer, Elizabeth Norton, writes that "Anne was universally loved."
Anne of Cleves' motto "God Send Me Well to Keep" seems to be still relevant to those who cherish her memory.

From the diary of Hans Holbein the Younger, court painter of Henry VIII. Cleves, Germany - summer, 1539

It is a special joy to paint a portrait of Anne of Cleves, Duke William's sister. She told me yesterday that she was born on September 22, 1515 in Dusseldorf, in this German duchy of Cleves. Her father was Duke John III, a Protestant and her mother, Duchess Maria of Julich, is Catholic. Anne seems to be pious but relaxed (not dogmatic at all) about religious matters.

Although King Henry VIII has commissioned me to paint a portrait of Anne of Cleves and his minister, Thomas Cromwell, is urging this Protestant alliance, neither of them have met Anne or know her real feelings. She has been told by Christopher Mont, the English ambassador in Cleves, that King Henry VIII is handsome, generous and kind. This innocent lady will soon discover the painful facts when she goes to England. I can only pray for her survival.

Do I know Anne of Cleves? Somewhat but much remains a mystery about this future Queen of England.

As a painter, I capture on canvas the character, as well as the appearance, of those whose portraits I paint. I am fascinated by Anne of Cleves and I hope my work will evoke admiration for her.

Cleves, Germany - Late summer, 1539

Yesterday as I was finishing her portrait, Anne of Cleves asked me: "Will this picture please your king?" I replied: 'Why one king? Future generations of men will mourn that they were born too late to be the lover of Anna von Clef."

Let me now paint with words a portrait of Anne of Cleves/Anna von Clef.

Am I in love with her? Yes and no. I have carnally "known" many women. However, any gesture of intimacy towards my future queen will cost me my life. The horror of Anne Boleyn's trial and execution and that of her lovers, haunt me (and many) still. I can control my outer words, gestures and even expressions but my heart and soul know the truth of love.

Anne of Cleves fills my soul with joy and my heart with tenderness. Her presence evokes inspiration, not lust, delight but not greed.

Can you imagine a spring dawn near a beautiful mountain in the countryside? She is like a clear river, a pail of fresh milk, a green meadow! Her presence removes lust while her beauty and grace evoke admiration and awe!

When I watch her sewing, her long, firm fingers embroidering an altar cloth, inwardly I become a child again, innocent and good, in spite of all the wine and women I have tasted in my life. All this sounds strange, but it is true! How would I describe Anne succinctly? A golden lily! She is a maiden of twenty-four. But she knows not what will befall her body once she marries Great Harry! I am a loyal servant of the King, our sovereign lord. I am honored to be his court painter BUT my heart aches and breaks for Anne of Cleves! It would be treason to breathe even a word of caution to her. I can only pray that God will save this lovely lady's life!

From the diary of Anna von Clef: Cleves - summer, 1539

Master Holbein, King Henry VIII's court painter, arrived in Cleves yesterday. I had told my brother, William, The Duke of Cleves, that the absence of jewels and court dress in my closet make it impossible for me to sit for a formal portrait. In spite of my objections, Master-Holbein has persuaded me to sit for this portrait which he began today. He has told me that the silver cross on a chain which I wear and my red dress will suffice.

There is magic in Master Holbein's fingers! The face on his canvas is truly mine, but my simple dress looks gorgeous! The artist tells me that King Henry VIII will love this portrait. Furthermore, Master Holbein says that when I am Queen of England, Anna Regina, the king will give me a royal wardrobe. If that is true, then my face is my fortune! Yes, the painting is an exact replica of me, like a mirror! Only the dress is beautified, not my face (or form).

From the diary of Anna von Clef: Cleves - late summer, 1539

Master Holbein has almost finished my portrait. I have chosen as my insignia the swan symbol of Cleves and the motto: "God send me well to keep." Master Holbein and I have become friends. We laugh together sometimes. Once he even tried to teach me a dance of the English court. Then he said: "The King's grace has hurt his leg in a riding accident. His leg has a wound which is healing slowly. Can you put herbs and plaster on it? The wound has a rank smell. Can you wash his sore leg and bandage it? Perhaps it would be best if you danced not at all. Simply tell him: 'Sire, I know not dancing. Let me sit by you."

I asked him: "Master Holbein, the English ambassador here, tells me this king loves music. Shall I sing or play the lute?" He answered: "Dear Lady, feign ignorance of everything - music, dancing and theology; even of card games. The King is attracted by innocence which you have and ignorance which you will pretend to have. Let him be your master and mentor in everything. Tell him you know nothing and he knows everything. That will please this king."

I know how to run a household. I like sewing, embroidery, and gardening. I love birds and dogs. I enjoy reading books of history and following current events. Maybe I can surprise Great Harry by proving to him that I can discuss politics and affairs of state in an intelligent way. Master Holbein did <u>not</u> ask me to feign ignorance of the topics I have mentioned above. I intend to learn English quickly, since the King knows no German. I have but a little Latin now but I will learn that also.

From the diary of 'Mother Lowe," the chaperone of Anne of Cleves: November, 1539

The mother of Anne of Cleves, Duchess Maria, has asked me to accompany her daughter and her maids of honor to England. We will take the overland route to Calais (the English colony in France), then journey by sea across the English Channel to Deal in Kent, England. Then we will go by carriage to Rochester, finally to Greenwich to meet the King.

From the diary of "Mother Lowe:" December, 1559, Calais

We are now in Calais, very hospitably entertained by Lord and Lady Lisle. Her daughter Anne Basset will be one of Anne of Cleves' ladies-in-waiting. There are rumors that Anne Basset is a mistress of the king. Lady Lisle speaks well of her future queen and wrote to her daughter that Anne would be "good and gentle to serve and please."

There have been severe winter storms which have delayed our passage to England. The English king has sent his own Lord High Admiral, the Earl of Southampton with various courtiers, including the two brothers of the late queen, Jane Seymour, to escort Anne of Cleves to England. While waiting for these

4

December storms to end, the English Admiral has been teaching Anne card games (one is called Sent) that King Henry enjoys.

My hands are full! The ducal family of Cleves wanted to make a good impression. They have sent a retinue of three hundred and fifty people from Germany to accompany Anne to England. One hundred members of this vast retinue are Anne's personal servants who include her twelve ladies in waiting, a doctor, a cook, a secretary, household officers and an artist, Suzanne Horenbout. Cleves has also sent many members of its aristocracy and its ambassadors in this retinue. The agreement is that most of the people in this large group will return to Germany, after the wedding.

From the diary of "Mother Lowe:" December 27, 1539

We reached England today, landing in Deal, Kent. The English king's old friend and former brother-in-law, the Duke of Suffolk and his very young second wife were waiting to greet us. They escorted Anne and her retinue to Dover Castle where we spent the night.

December 29, 1539

We arrived in Canterbury, the center of the Church of England. Its ancient cathedral is impressive! Anne was greeted by Archbishop Cranmer himself.

From" Mother Lowe's" diary - December 31, 1539

From Canterbury we rode to Sittingbourne and thence to Rochester, escorted by the Duke of Norfolk. Here I locked horns with Lady Browne who is in charge of Anne's English ladies-in-waiting. These six English ladies have been selected by the King himself. They are Lady Margaret Douglas, the King's niece,

The Duchesses of Richmond and Suffolk, the Countess of Sussex, Lady Howard and Lady Clinton. (The last lady is the King's former mistress, Bessie Blount.)

Lady Browne, in order to offend me, spoke very rudely of Anne of Cleves. She said that there was in Anne "such fashion and manner of bringing up so gross and far discrepant from the King's Highness' appetite." What nonsense! Anne of Cleves is a model of good behavior and modesty, so different from the aristocratic sluts and hussies of this English court. Anne and I are pretending not to understand English which we have studied well during the last six months in order to hear what the English are really saying about us. For example, they don't like German dresses. They laughed at the garments of Anne's twelve ladies and said they "dressed after a fashion so heavy and tasteless that it would make them appear frightful even if they were beauties." Well, if the truth be told, I would say the same about the vulgar dresses of these English high-born sluts. So there!

However, the people of good judgment in the English court have spoken well of Anne of Cleves. They said her "manner is like a princess." They have also noticed her kindness and gentleness and are suitably impressed.

From the diary of Anne of Cleves - December 31, 1539,

Rochester, England

Now that I am in England, I will use the English version of my name, Anne of Cleves. A new year will start tomorrow and with it a new life for me here in England. I hear that I will be married soon and then I will truly become the Queen of England. King Henry's children - what will they think of me? I am so ready to love them! The Lady Mary and I are the same age, twenty-four. I am only a few months older than the daughter of King Henry's first Queen, the late Katherine of Aragon! Lady Elizabeth, the daughter of King Henry's second wife, the executed Anne Boleyn, is seven and Prince Edward, the late Queen Jane Seymour's son, is two years old. I shall love them all!

The reason for my marriage is not only to secure the Protestant alliance with Germany (and thus protect England from the Catholic powers of Spain and France) but I am to be impregnated by this unknown king in order to bear him sons. I am a young, healthy virgin and my main function in this marriage is to have boys and more boys.

My expression is crest-fallen now and my face is pale, not from the Channel crossing but from fear. I have heard enough to know that my prospective husband is a ruthless despot. I am about to marry a monster!

From the diary of Anne of Cleves: January 1, 1540 - Rochester, England

This New Year has had a very strange start! It is very late at night now but I want to write down today's events while they are still fresh in my memory.

This afternoon I was looking out of the window of this palace at New Year's pageants when the door of my private chamber burst open. Six men, all dressed alike, came in unannounced. The oldest, largest and tallest man in this group clasped me to his bosom saying they were all sent by King Henry VIII to welcome me to England! I extricated myself from that unwanted embrace, told the man to thank his king and pointed to the window, outside which a pageant was taking place. The tall man looked angry and limped out of the room, followed by the other five men. I could not help but notice that the whole room was filled with a foul stench emanating from the tall man's leg which had a big bandage on it. Soon, the chamber door opened again and the tall, fat man, now dressed in royal purple, re-entered the room and was introduced to me as my future husband, King Henry VIII. He said he had come to Rochester to see me and to "nourish love." I sank into a deep courtesy but I was silent with surprise. My discomfort and physical disgust must have been obvious to the king. I bowed my head in submission but I could not smile. He did not embrace me again but took my hand and we retired to a small room beyond that vast chamber. King Henry VIII told me that England now had no need of an alliance with Cleves. The French king, Francis the First, had sent him a Christmas gift. That meant that France and Spain were no longer close allies and the danger of a Catholic coalition against England was over. He asked me if there was an impediment to our upcoming marriage. I told him that I had once been betrothed to the son of the Duke of Lorraine but that "pre-contract" had long been cancelled.

With the mental clarity born of fear, based on my recent knowledge of King Henry's dreadful treatment of his first two wives, Katherine of Aragon and Anne Boleyn, I offered him a solution. "Sire, let our marriage proceed," I said "but you should tell everyone immediately that my appearance is not to your liking. This marriage can be dissolved if we do not have physical relations. Tell them also that there is an unpleasant smell in the room. We know it comes from your leg. But let the courtiers think you imagine it comes from my body or my clothes. Our marriage can then be annulled."

Amazed and grateful, Henry VIII gave me a new title "the King's good sister." He said that I had shown more sense than his first two wives. He also said he would reward me liberally with money and property if I lived in England. The King told me that I would have royal precedence over all English women with the exception of his future queen (if he remarried) and his daughters, Mary and Elizabeth. The whole process would take six more months and then I would be a royal lady of independent means. How could I refuse? Returning to Cleves as a rejected bride, living on my brother's charity while he arranged another marriage for me as a diplomatic pawn to another stranger? No! I chose to live in England as the honored sister of its generous and grateful king! Having settled everything to our mutual advantage, the king gave me a brotherly peck on my cheek and left the room.

From the diary of Edward Hall, Courtier - January, 1540

On January 2, 1540, Henry VIII moved with the court to Greenwich where the wedding is to take place. Anne of Cleves went to Dartford Palace where she spent the night. The next day she rode in procession to Shooters Hill (on January 3, 1540). There she was welcomed by the Earl of Rutland and officers and great ladies of the English court. Anne of Cleves was wearing a round gown of cloth of gold, cut in the Dutch fashion without a train and a headdress covered with pearls and other rich stones. She was ready for her official reception by the king at Blackheath.

On Blackheath, near London, the Mayor and Corporation of London, knights, soldiers, livened servants, gentlemen, pensioners, as well as German merchants arranged themselves in orderly ranks. At noon, to the sound of trumpets, the King rode through Greenwich Park towards the waiting crowds. Norfolk, Suffolk and Cranmer, the King's many officers, the gentlemen of the Privy Chamber, barons, bishops, earls, foreign ambassadors, the Lord Privy Seal, the Lord Chancellor, nobles and bishops were all part of the King's retinue. Great Harry wore a cloak of purple velvet, many jewels and was riding a fine horse, Even the King's saddle was covered with embroidered, jeweled cloth of gold. King Henry was followed by the Lord Chamberlain, the Master of Horse, Pages of Honor and the Yeoman of the Guard. The king came near the pavilions and waited.

Soon Anne of Cleves rode toward the King who "put off his bonnet and came toward her, and with most lovely countenance and princely behavior, saluted, welcomed and embraced her, to the great rejoicing of the beholders. Anne with most amiable aspect and womanly behavior, received His Grace with many sweet words and great thanks and praising."

The royal couple rode back to Greenwich followed by their huge retinue. As they approached Greenwich Palace, they could see many Londoners rowing up and down the River Thames in decorated barges from which issued music and songs praising Henry and Anne, which pleased the royal pair. The King and Anne of Cleves dismounted in the outer court of Greenwich Palace. Then "the King lovingly embraced and kissed her, bidding her welcome to her own, and led her by the arm through the hall, and brought her up to her privy chamber, where he left her for that time."

Meanwhile "a great peal of guns" was fired in Anne's honor. That night the King hosted a magnificent banquet in Anne's honor.

On the morning of Epiphany, January 6, 1540 the King emerged from his private chamber and spoke to his Lord Privy Seal, Thomas Cromwell. Our sovereign lord was about to wed Anne of Cleves in Greenwich Palace in the Queen's closet. The King told Cromwell just before the wedding "My Lord, if it were not to satisfy the world, and My Realm, I would not do that I must do this day for none earthly thing."

At 8:00 a.m. on January 6, 1540 the King and his nobles went to the gallery that led to the royal closets. He waited there having sent some lords to fetch Anne of Cleves. The king was richly attired in a garment of "cloth of gold raised with great flowers of silver, furred with black beneath a cloak of crimson satin embroidered with large diamonds." He also wore a collar covered with jewels, around his neck.

Anne of Cleves came towards the King. Her bridal attire was "a gown of rich cloth of silver set full of large flowers of great Orient pearl, made after the Dutch fashion, with jeweled collar and belt. Her long, golden hair was loose beneath a gem-studded coronal of gold with trefoils fashioned to represent sprigs of rosemary." Rosemary represented remembrance, constancy and virginity.

Our new queen was preceded by the English nobles and escorted by two German lords. She came to the gallery and made three low curtseys to the King. They were married by Archbishop Cranmer. Around the wedding ring of Anne of Cleves was inscribed her motto: "*God send me well to keep.*" After the wedding, the royal couple went hand in hand to the King's closet to hear Mass. Then they drank spiced wine. After that, the King then went to his privy chamber while the new Queen was escorted to her chamber by the Dukes of Norfolk and Suffolk, At 9 a.m. the King rejoined the Queen. He was attired in a robe of rich tissue lined with crimson velvet. Then "with her sergeant-of-arms and all her officers before her, like a queen, the King and she went openly in procession" into the King's chamber. In the afternoon, the Queen changed into a gown with sables, long fitted sleeves and a jeweled headdress. Then, she accompanied the King to Vespers and later they dined together. Afterwards there were "banquets, masques and diverse disports till the time came that it pleased the King and her to take their rest."

From the diary of Anne of Cleves: January 7, 1540

Last night the King and I had a very unusual wedding night. There was no public bedding ceremony such as occurred during his three previous marriages.

Also, the headboard of the bed designed for us has erotic carvings with the intertwined initials H and A. This bed was carved last year, 1539. I did not sleep in that bed. The King slept there, fully dressed. I was also fully dressed. I sat in a chair near the window and dozed for a short time at daybreak. I even wore my headdress and my hair (which I wore loose during my marriage ceremony as a sign of my virginity) was hidden from view, lest it excite Great Harry. I had fragrant herbs burning in the fire with the wood to perfume the bedroom. Thus the "displeasant" smell of the King's leg wound was kept from overpowering the room.

My terror of a sexual initiation by this terrible old man is laid to rest.

Last night I sat still in my chair, at some distance from the King who was reclining on the bed. I reminded him more than once that it was of the utmost political advantage to him to leave our brief marriage unconsummated. I told the King I would confirm in writing that this is the case. Then our marriage would definitely be annulled, leaving him free to follow his heart. I told him that I have noticed the Duke of Norfolk's niece, Catherine Howard. She is a lovely English girl of seventeen or eighteen (as opposed to my twenty-four years of age) who would be a delicious bride and a fertile wife for him. That would appease Henry's Catholic courtiers like Norfolk and Gardiner and please the Kings of France and Spain. The King was happy to hear my words. He even said that as Catherine Howard's king, he could bed her before he decided to wed her.

In spite of Great Harry's ruthlessness (especially when opposed) and fierce greed for money and property, there is still a strong streak of chivalry and generosity in him. He told me that pretending to others that I am an unwanted bride is distasteful to him. But he will follow my advice for both our sakes. He said he will safeguard my virginity, so that both of us could truthfully state that our marriage was unconsummated and should be annulled.

From the diary of Anne of Cleves: January 10, 1540

Great Harry has taken my advice and told Thomas Cromwell, his Lord Privy Seal, the High Admiral of England, the Earl of Southampton (who came to Calais to escort me to England), the courtier Anthony Denny, even the King's doctors Chamber and Butts that although he is very virile with other women, he cannot bring himself to consummate his marriage with me because he finds me physically unattractive. I am only sorry that Master Holbein has temporarily fallen from royal favor because he painted a true portrait of my beauty. However, King Henry has promised to send money to Holbein secretly and to restore him as his court painter once my marriage is dissolved.

From the diary of Anne of Cleves - January 11, 1540

Earlier today the King and I presided over a tournament in "honor of our nuptials." For the first time I wore an English gown with a French hood which is fashionable here. The King quietly complemented me on my appearance.

From the diary of Anne of Cleves - February 3, 1540

Instead of engaging in the expensive ceremony of coronation for me, the King has arranged for me to make a state entry into Westminster tomorrow, February 4. He will sail with me in the royal barge from Greenwich, attended by the nobility and guildsmen in smaller barges.

From the diary of Anne of Cleves - February 4, 1540

All went smoothly today as planned. I received a "thunderous salute" from the guns in the Tower of London as the King and I sailed past the Tower. The good citizens of London lined the banks of the Thames River and cheered and waved to us. At Westminster stairs, the King helped me out of the royal barge and he and I walked in procession to Whitehall Palace.

Great Harry told me that the state apartments of St. James's Palace are now ready for us and the Chapel Royal is nearing completion. I have already been shown its magnificent ceiling, painted by Holbein. This Tudor ceiling celebrates my marriage to the King and our initials, mottoes, badges and the date 1540 are inscribed on the ceiling. This new chapel will now be the official home of the Chapel Royal.

From the diary of Anne Cleves - May 5, 1540

My last public appearance as the Queen of England ended today. On May Day, the King and I watched the usual May celebrations and jousts from the new gatehouse at Whitehall. This tournament lasted for five days. When it ended today, the King and I attended a banquet at Durham House. To my surprise, the public were admitted so that they could watch the King giving money and grants of houses to the victors of the jousts.

During this brief period of queenship, I have done my best to be a good example of moral virtue to all my subjects, a generous patron to my staff, and a pleasant friend to the King.

My brother William, the Duke of Cleves, is inclined to Lutheranism. The King's oldest daughter, the Lady Mary, is my age but a staunch Roman Catholic. She has been alarmed by my marriage to her father, fearing that Lutheranism will prevail in England. On the contrary, I have dutifully observed here all the rites and rituals of the Church of England which is under the King's authority.

My clothes are now English gowns (with French hoods which are fashionable in the English court). I prefer gowns of black satin or damask which compliment my fair skin and golden hair. Some of my new jewels are designed by Master Holbein and feature the entwined initials H and A. Recently I purchased a diamond brooch with a Biblical theme.

I am told by my ladies that though the King is kind to me, he does not lavish jewels and castles on me, as he did on his previous wives.

But, I have no complaints. He gave me Baynard's Castle for my jointure, some jewels, plenty of money for clothes and other expenses.

Only two of my German maids, Katherine and Gertrude have been allowed to stay in England under the supervision of Mother Lowe. However, I have many English ladies who seek to serve me. I particularly enjoy the company of the Countess of Rutland, Lady Rochford and Lady Edgecombe whom I address as Eleanor, Jane and Winifred, respectively.

I have come to share the King's love of music and I have found some fine musicians whom I employ to entertain him. Among my musicians are members of the Jewish Italian Bassano family who recently arrived in the English court in the spring of 1540.

I love the palace gardens and I pay my gardeners well. I love needlework, specially a form of German cross-stitch. I have learned to play cards and to enjoy English ale (an occasional glass). I also love watching visiting acrobats.

One of the King's courtiers bought a lovely green parrot from a sailor and gave it to me as a special gift. My other pet is a brown and white, small spaniel who came with me from Cleves.

From the diary of Anne Cleves May, 1540

I have ordered a red velvet bonnet with a white feather for two year old Prince Edward, my step-son. I have met the Lady Elizabeth who is seven. Her gravity (and ability to write serious letters) is far beyond her years. I am teaching her embroidery with German designs. I sense great reserve from the Lady Mary, the King's oldest daughter. Since we are the same age, I hope we can be friends. I have already told her that my marriage will be dissolved. She also knows that my mother, the Duchess Maria, is a Roman Catholic. She seemed relieved to know that my marriage to her father was not consummated, so no child of mine will compete with her for the English throne.

My English is fluent now. But I draw a line at some things. Let my paid musicians entertain the King and his court! I am not Anne Boleyn. I do not wish to sing or play musical instruments publicly. Also, I will not expose by breasts in the fashionable style of this court. My dresses are beautiful English gowns with modest designs.

From the diary of Edward Hall, courtier - February through July, 1540

I heard that Lady Lisle of Calais had sent in February, 1540, a large bribe (I don't know what it is) to Anne of Cleves' confidante Mother Lowe, hoping to get her daughter Katherine into the new Queen's household. However, King Henry VIII has made it clear that no new maids of honor will be accepted until one of the present ladies leaves to get married. In March, 1540 Lord Lisle was accused of mismanaging his duties in Calais and is now imprisoned in the Tower of London. However, his daughter, Anne Basset, continues to serve Queen Anne of Cleves and enjoys the King's favor.

By April, 1540, King Henry was resolved to end his marriage to Anne of Cleves. He has declared "before God that she is not his lawful wife." A complaint English Parliament has asked the King to examine the circumstances of his fourth marriage which appears not to be valid.

Thomas Cromwell, the chief advocate of the King's marriage to Anne of Cleves, has been ordered by the King to approach the Parliament and *"to undo it."*

In recognition of his compliance, on April 17, 1540, his Majesty raised Cromwell to the peerage, as the Earl of Essex and also appointed him to the post of Lord Great Chamberlain of England.

Cromwell engineered the execution of Anne Boleyn and her lovers and arranged the Dissolution of the Monasteries and the transfer of church wealth to the King's coffers. Yes, he has been a very useful servant to the King. However, Cromwell has many enemies. The English Catholic nobility, led by the Duke of Norfolk and Gardiner, is trying to influence the King to overthrow and execute Cromwell.

Their most powerful pawn is Norfolk's beautiful young niece, Catherine Howard. It is whispered that this lovely young girl is not a maiden but well experienced in lovemaking. However, the King is blinded by Catherine Howard's youth and beauty. He dotes on her and showers her with expensive gifts. It is widely rumored that he has slept with her. She is a pretty, plump girl with auburn hair, of small stature but very graceful. The Spanish ambassador (still devoted to King Henry's first queen, the Spanish princess, Katherine of Aragon), describes Catherine Howard as *"imperious and willful."* Catherine Howard is the protege of her uncle the Duke of Norfolk and the other English Catholics. But I don't think she has any interest in religion. She loves jewels and pretty dresses and flattery. The King adores Catherine Howard calling her his *"rose without a thorn."* Can Catherine Howard really give up handsome young men?

The terrible fate of her cousin Anne Boleyn should frighten Catherine Howard into complete fidelity to the King. But can her empty head and hot, young body follow the path of prudence?

What amazes and puzzles us all in the English court is the continuing cheerful composure of Anne of Cleves. She seems to be untouched by the events around her. She and the King behave more like affectionate siblings than man and wife! This German lady has adapted very well to our English ways and is greatly loved by the common people who are the backbone of England.

Excerpts from Edward Hall's diary - June and July, 1540

On June 10, Thomas Cromwell was arrested without warning. This amazed most people here, especially Cromwell, who believed that he had reached the peak of his career. The Duke of Norfolk and the Earl of Southampton stripped him of his insignia and seal and he was imprisoned in the Tower of London. On June 29, Parliament passed an Act of Attainder condemning Cromwell as a traitor and heretic. Richard Rich, who had testified (falsely, many think) against Sir Thomas More, now spoke against Cromwell. The Duke of Norfolk is the chief architect of Cromwell's downfall.

Archbishop Cranmer bravely asked the King:

"Who shall Your Grace trust hereafter if you may not trust him (Cromwell)?" But Great Harry ignored Cranmer.

The King did not put Cromwell to death immediately. He rightly believed that Cromwell could help to dissolve the Cleves marriage. As soon as Cromwell complied with suitable information, the marriage of Anne of Cleves was annulled on July 9, 1540 by convocation of all representatives of the Church and State of England with King Henry as the head. The grounds for annulling this marriage were the King's lack of consent to his fourth marriage and Anne's alleged pre contract with the son of the Duke of Lorraine.

Earlier on June 24, 1540, King Henry VIII sent Anne of Cleves to Richmond Palace, "for her health, open air and pleasure." The following day, a group of the King's counselors came to tell her that her marriage was null and void. She agreed, sent the King a letter of submission and she returned Baynard's Castle to him. King Henry VIII rewarded her with a generous financial settlement plus the gifts of Richmond Palace, Hever Castle, the manor of Bletchingly and the right to call herself "the King's good sister," with precedence over all English ladies except the Queen (should the King remarry) and the King's daughters. She was also allowed to keep all her clothes, tapestries, plates and jewels and given a comfortable household composed mainly of her German servants, to her great joy.

Anne wrote to her brother, the Duke of Cleves: "God willing, I propose to lead my life in this realm."

Grateful to Anne of Cleves for her compliance in ending their marriage, King Henry has become an affectionate brother to her calling her, "my beloved sister Anna" and visiting her at Richmond Palace.

Anne of Cleves looks very happy and wears a new gown every day. She is esteemed as "the King's good sister," and has established a reputation as a gracious hostess and a generous patron to all who serve her.

Edward Hall's diary continues - summer, 1540

What a strange day! Thomas Cromwell was executed today (July 28, 1540) but very few people, if any, mourned him. There is also a strong, plausible rumor that King Henry VIII and Catherine Howard had a quiet wedding today in Oatlands Palace. The Bishop of London, Edmund Bonner is believed to have conducted the royal wedding. It is widely known that the King has specially commissioned an ornate bed, set with pearls on the headboard, from a French craftsman, for his nuptial chamber. He certainly lavishes ornaments on Catherine Howard who is as giddy as she is greedy and only enjoys merrymaking. I wonder what sort of queen and royal mother she will make? Of course, many allowances must be made. She is a girl of eighteen and the King is forty-nine! I heard that on August 8, 1540, the King will publicly announce his new marriage and Catherine Howard will be *"shown openly"* and prayed for as Queen in the Chapel Royal at Hampton Court.

Anne of Cleves seems serene and well, happy with her new life, in Richmond Palace.

From the diary of Anne of Cleves: 1540 --1552.

In July, 1540, I had written to my brother the Duke of Cleves that I wished to remain in England as the sister of King Henry VIII and that "*I am very content and I wish you and my mother should know this ... "*

On August 6, 1540 the King (who had married Catherine Howard a few days ago) came to Richmond Palace to dine with me. He wished to assure me of his continuing brotherly affection and esteem. He also wanted to see for himself that my new household arrangements were fully satisfactory to me. We had a long, friendly conversation. He assured me that as long as I chose to live in England, I could dwell here in peace and plenty with royal privileges, as the King's *"good sister."*

On January 3, 1541 I came to the King's court bearing with me New Year's gifts for Great Harry and his fifth queen, Catherine Howard. I gave them two beautiful horses with saddles of purple velvet. The King bowed to me and gave me a brotherly kiss. The Queen (who had been one of my ladies in waiting) welcomed me with warmth, as I knelt before her. That evening and the following night, I dined with the King and Queen and we talked and laughed. On both nights, after the King retired, the Queen and I danced together. Furthermore, with his approval, the Queen gave me a ring and two lap dogs -- presents which the King had given her. Altogether, 1541 was a very Happy New Year!

The French ambassador to England at that time was Marillac. He reported to the French king that I appeared to be "*joyous and content*" which was (and is) very true!

The following New Year, 1542, the King and I exchanged gifts. He gave me some pots and flagons for my household and I gave him some rich, crimson velvet.

There was much speculation from Cleves and elsewhere that I would be reinstated as the Queen of England after the arrest and execution of Catherine Howard in November, 1541.However, I firmly denied all such allegations.

In March, 1543 at the King's invitation, I spent three days at his court. The Spanish Imperial ambassador seemed uncomfortable at my continued presence in England.

When I heard that the King married, on July 12, 1543, the twice widowed and childless Katherine Parr who was four years older than me, as his sixth wife, I did say that the new queen "*was not nearly as beautiful as me.*" I was simply stating a fact without jealousy.

Later that month (July 1543) the King came to dine with me at Richmond Palace. He told me that he always enjoyed visiting me.

In the summer of 1546, I returned to the King's court for another delightful visit.

From July, 1540 when we were divorced, until his death in January, 1547, King Henry VIII was unfailingly kind and generous to me. He often came to dine with me in Richmond Palace, wrote to me in his own hand, invited me to his court and gave me much money and property. In addition to Richmond Palace, Hever Castle and Beltchingly Manor, he gave me estates called Kemsing and Deal in the English countryside. Among his letters and papers you will find documents written in his own hand which are entitled "*expenses for my beloved sister Anna.*"

Due to the generosity of King Henry VIII, I was even able to send my brother expensive presents such as horses and greyhounds, in the autumn of 1546. In 1547, the interference of my brother, the Duke of Cleves, resulted in the loss of three of my German servants. He wished to plant his own spies into my household, being an inquisitive and greedy man. I forgive him, my conscience is clear.

His courtiers informed me that the King had died in January, 1547. Of course, my household and I immediately went into deep mourning.

King Henry's son Edward is now our King. The boy is fond of me and I of him. However, the men who govern England for him, including his Seymour uncles. are greedy and cruel. These counselors of King Edward VI have confiscated Richmond Palace and Bletchingly Manor which King Henry VIII had granted me for life. After I stood up to them, these men in power have given me two lesser estates in Kent, Penshurst and Dartford Priory. The latter is a small, comfortable house which had once belonged to a church. By 1552, I was so tired of the meanness of the royal councilors that I was thinking of returning to Cleves, much to the dismay of my brother the duke who would then have to financially support me.

In 1551, I enjoyed a visit with King Henry's daughter, Princess Mary. We are close in age and over the years we had come to love and trust each other. I told her that the Spanish Ambassador, Simon Renard, was mistaken in regarding me as a German Protestant spy. Renard was spreading rumors that if the strongly Catholic Princess Mary ascended the

English throne, I would plot with my brother, the Duke of Cleves, to support the Protestant cause by backing King Henry's other daughter, Elizabeth.

During this visit in 1551, I did tell Princess Mary that I had always been a loyal "sister" to her father and a loving "aunt" to her brother. Moreover, we are all worried about the health of King Edward VI.

As next in succession, if Princess Mary ascended the English throne, I assured her of my complete loyalty. I also told her about my own religious practices. Princess Mary's Spanish mother, Queen Katherine of Aragon and my mother Duchess Maria of Julich and Cleves were staunch Catholics. Hence, I have found solace in the Catholic religion.

Recently, in the spring of 1551, I have secretly become a Catholic. Neither the very Protestant boy King Edward VI nor his royal council know of my conversion. To survive in Tudor England, I said as little as possible, in public and in private.

Princess Mary was delighted to hear what I told her. She promised me her whole-hearted support.

I had been both surprised and saddened when King Henry VIII's widow Katherine Parr (who had married Jane Seymour's brother, Admiral Thomas Seymour) died in 1548 giving birth to a daughter.

From the diary of Anne of Cleves: 1553-1557

I was not surprised but very sad when young King Edward VI died in 1553. He was succeeded by his half-sister the Princess Mary.

On September 29, 1553, I rode in a coach with Princess Elizabeth. We entered London together to attend the coronation for Queen Mary I. I sat with Princess Elizabeth and Queen Mary at the same royal table for the coronation banquet. This was my last public appearance as a member of the royal family of England.

However, I have always remained in close touch with Queen Mary I. She continues to be my gracious and generous friend, much more a sister to me than to Princess Elizabeth whom she suspects of heresy and treason.

Thanks to Queen Mary, I am living in Chelsea Manor, the former home of Sir Thomas More who lost his life for his support of Queen Katherine of Aragon and her daughter, our sovereign lady.

Chelsea Manor is a delightful residence, near the Thames River, not far from London.

Thank God, I can now openly practice Roman Catholicism. I also know that Queen Mary will continue to love and believe in me no matter what false rumors about me are circulated by the Spanish Imperial ambassador and others.

What of the Princess Elizabeth, the daughter of King Henry VIII and Anne Boleyn? She is now (July 1557) almost twenty four years old. I have known her since she was seven years old, a precocious child. Elizabeth's health is delicate. She is prone to severe headaches and stomach pains. Her build is lean and wiry. She has the reserved, oval face of her paternal grandfather, King Henry VII, the Welshman who founded the Tudor dynasty. Elizabeth is living quietly in Hatfield, in the English countryside. She is a shrewd and scholarly young woman. During the reign of her father, King Henry VIII, she was his *obedient and devoted* Bess. During the reign of her late half brother King Edward VI, she styled herself his *sweet sister*

Temperance. Now, during the reign of Elizabeth's half-sister, the Catholic Queen Mary I, *Elizabeth is biding her time.*

It is important for all of us to remember that our sovereign lady is the granddaughter of Spain's warrior queen, Isabella of Castile (who was also the patroness of Christopher Columbus) and the daughter of King Henry VIII's saintly first wife, Katherine of Aragon.

Elizabeth knows that if she becomes openly Catholic, many English people will be displeased. If she defies Queen Mary I, Elizabeth could lose her place in the succession and be imprisoned for heresy and treason. So, she bides her time, watched closely by Queen Mary's spies.

Queen Mary has had a sad life! She longs to secure the succession with a Catholic heir to the English throne.

But she has not yet borne a child. Moreover, her marriage to her cousin, King Philip of Spain (a cold hearted man, over a decade younger than her and a known womanizer) has undermined the Queen's popularity in England. Years of persecution by her father, King Henry VIII, has left Queen Mary badly wounded. I can only hope and pray that Queen Mary's many good qualities of head and heart will be kindly remembered by the historians of her reign, now and in the future.

I hope that Elizabeth has learned some valuable lessons from observing my life! By remaining a maiden lady and keeping myself free of religious, romantic and political intrigues, I am independently wealthy, due to the generosity of Great Harry and his heirs to the English throne!

I have always acted on my conviction that it is better to follow the path of gentle firmness and tact. I have rejected impatience and force, believing that water, in time can erode a stone while a sword can be turned against oneself, by a foe. *Time has been my ally. I do hope that Elizabeth has learned useful lessons by observing my life!*

Having done all I could for Great Harry's three children, for my English and German household staff, over these sixteen and a half years (January 1540 to July 1557), it is almost time for me to exchange earthly for eternal life, through God's grace.

I have settled my affairs and made my will. I am ready to face my Maker. Many important events have occurred in my life and in England since King Henry VIII adopted me as his "beloved sister Anna" in July,

1540 when our brief marriage ended. Since I am nearing the end of my earthly life, I have put pen to paper and written down a synopsis of my understanding of these events. I have tried to leave an accurate summary of the facts.

Although I am only forty one years of age, (July 1557) I have a "declining illness." God willing, I want to die with a peaceful heart and a mind and soul filled with prayer. Concluding this diary will free my mind of all earthly concerns.

From the diary of Anne of Cleves: July 16, 1557.

My will was written during the last two days. I have bequeathed my best jewels to "*our most dearest and entirely beloved sovereign lady, Queen Mary.*" Her majesty will be the overseer of my will. I have left my second best jewel to King Henry's other daughter, Elizabeth whom I have asked to care for Dorothy Curzen, one of my maids. I have also left jewelry for my brother and his wife, the Duke and Duchess of Cleves, for Lady Suffolk, for the Countess of Arundel, for Lord Paget and for my cousin Waldeck. I have made bequests to all my servants, English and German and to the poor who are my special beneficiaries. I have requested to receive the rites and blessing of the" Holy Church according to the Catholic faith wherein we end our life in this transitory world." The executors of my will are the Archbishop of York, the Earl of Arundel, Sir Edward Peckham and Sir Richard Preston.

Queen Mary has promised me that my body will be buried in Westminster Abbey with royal honors. The Queen has tearfully assured me that there will be a Requiem Mass for me. Moreover, a banquet to honor my memory, will be hosted by my chief mourner, Elizabeth Paulet, the Marchioness of Winchester and her husband at their London home.

By and large, I have had a peaceful and pleasant life here in England. I have been a kind and caring mistress to all who served me. I have been a gracious hostess and a joyful, generous presence to everyone who entered my life. I have always been a loving servant of God Almighty.

Peacefully, I bid farewell to my earthly life and I am radiantly ready for Heaven.

As my final gift, I would like this book to end with the words of Fra. Giovanni, an Italian monk. He wrote the following letter as a Christmas present to a friend in 1513, two years before I was born. This letter has been my guiding star over the years. I pray that Fra. Giovanni's luminous words will fill your soul with joy and peace!

God be with thee and me all ways, always, all days .... Amen.

Anne of Cleves

Take Joy!

Letter from Fra. Giovanni, 1513

I am your friend
and my love for you goes deep.
there is nothing I can give you
which you have not got,
but there is much, very much
that while I cannot give it,
you can take.

No heaven can come to us
unless our hearts find rest in today.
Take heaven!
No peace lies in the future
which is not hidden
in this present little instant.
Take Peace!
The gloom of the world is but a
shadow.
Behind it,
yet within our reach
is joy.
Take Joy!

There is radiance and glory
in the darkness
could we but see –
and to see we have only to look.
I beseech you to look!

Life is so generous a giver,
but we, judging its gifts
by the covering,
cast them away as ugly,
or heavy or heard.
Remove the covering
and you will find beneath it
a living splendor,
woven of love,
by wisdom with power.

Welcome it, grasp it,
touch the angel's hand
that brings it to you.
everything we call a trial,
a sorrow, or a duty, believe me,
that angel's hand
is there,
the gift is there, and the wonder
of an overshadowing presence. Our
joys, too, be not
content with them as joys.
they, too, conceal diviner gifts.

Life is so full
of meaning and purpose,
so full of beauty
- beneath its covering-
that you will find earth
but cloaks your heaven.

Courage, then, to claim it,
that is all.
But courage you have,
and the knowledge that
we are all pilgrims together,
wending through
unknown country, home.

And so, at this time,
I greet you.
Not quite as the world
sends greetings,
but with profound esteem
and with the prayer
that for you
now and forever,
the day breaks
and the shadows flee away.

Primary Sources

1539 & 1540
Recorded by Eustace Chapuys
Spanish Ambassador

(Anne's reaction was undoubtedly a humbling experience for the King).

1539

This year on St. John's Day, 27th December, Lady Anne, daughter of the Duke of Cleves in Germany, landed at Dover at 5 o'clock at night, and there was honorably received by the Duke of Suffolk and other great lords, and so lodged at the castle. And on the following Monday she rode to Canterbury where she was honorably received by the Archbishop of Canterbury and other great men, and lodged at the King's palace at St. Austin's, and there highly feasted. On Tuesday, she came to Sittingbourne.

1540

On New Year's Eve the Duke of Norfolk and other knights and the barons of the exchequer received her grace on the heath, two miles beyond Rochester, and so brought her to the abbey of Rochester where she stayed that night and all New Year's Day, and on New Year's Day in the afternoon, the King's grace with five of his privy chamber, being disguised with mottled cloaks with hoods so that they should not be recognized, came secretly to Rochester, and so went up into the chamber where the said Lady Anne was looking out of a window to see the bull-baiting which was going on in the courtyard, and suddenly he embraced and kissed her, and showed her a token which the King had sent her for a New Year's gift, and she being abashed and not knowing who it was, thanked him, and so he spoke with her. But she regarded him little, but always looked out of the window....and when the King saw that she took so little notice of his coming, he went into another chamber and took off his cloak and came in again in a coat of purple velvet and when the lords and knights saw his grace, they did him reverence....and then her grace humbled herself lowly to the King's majesty, and his grace saluted her again, and they talked together lovingly, and afterwards

35

he took her by the hand and led her to another chamber where their graces amused themselves that night and on Friday until the afternoon.

.... So she came to Greenwich that night, and was received as queen. And the next day, being Sunday, the King's grace kept a great court at Greenwich, where his grace with the queen offered at mass, richly dressed. And on Twelfth Night which was Tuesday, the King's majesty was married to the said queen Anne solemnly, in her closet at Greenwich, and his grace and she went publicly in procession that day, she having a rich coronet of stones and pearls set with rosemary on her hair, and a gown of rich cloth of silver, richly hung with stones and pearls, with all her ladies and gentlewomen following her, which was a goodly sight to behold.

Letter of Anne of Cleves to her husband, King Henry VIII
11 July 1540

Background

The following letter was Anne of Cleves's very diplomatic response to Henry VIII's request for an annulment of their brief marriage. Though her brother pressed her to return home to the duchy of Cleves, Anne was content to remain in England. There were two reasons for this - first, Henry was so grateful for her easy submission and gracious manners, he rewarded her with a very comfortable lifestyle. She was able to live as a wealthy dowager and enjoyed a close relationship with the king (now termed her 'brother') and his three children. Secondly, she did not want to face an ignominious return to Cleves. After Henry's public rejection of their union, she would not have found another husband and would have been forced to rely on her brother's generosity.

Henry was very impressed by this letter. Its tone of respectful subservience to his wishes inspired his gratitude. Despite his reputation for tyranny, the great king could be kind and generous. Anne had little cause to think ill of him. After all, most historians focus on Henry's feelings in this matter - but perhaps the lady from Cleves was less than enamored with her husband and was equally desperate to escape the marriage. According to all reports, she learned to love English beer and grew plump and happy in her adopted country.

Pleaseth your most excellent majesty to understand that, whereas, at sundry times heretofore, I have been informed and perceived by certain lords and others of your grace's council, of the doubts and questions which have been moved and found in our marriage; and how hath petition thereupon been made to your highness by your nobles and commons, that the same might be examined and determined by the holy clergy of this realm; to testify to your highness by my writing, that which I have before promised by my word and will, that is to say, that the matter should be examined and determined by the said clergy; it may please your majesty to know that, though this case must needs be most hard and sorrowful unto me, for the great love which I bear to your most noble person, yet, having more regard to God and his truth than to any worldly affection, as it beseemed me, at the beginning, to submit me to such examination and determination of the said clergy, whom I have and do accept for judges competent in that behalf. So now being ascertained how the same clergy hath therein given their judgment and sentence, I acknowledge myself hereby to accept and approve the same, wholly and entirely putting myself, for my state and condition, to your highness' goodness and pleasure; most humbly beseeching your majesty that, though it be determined that the pretended matrimony between us is void and of none effect, whereby I neither can nor will repute myself for your grace's wife, considering this sentence (whereunto I stand) and your majesty's clean and pure living with me, yet it will please you to take me for one of your humble servants, and so determine of me, as I may sometimes have the fruition of your most noble presence; which as I shall esteem for a great benefit, so, my lords and others of your majesty's council, now being with me, have put me in comfort thereof; and that your highness will take me for your sister; for the which I most humbly thank you accordingly.

Thus, most gracious prince, I beseech our Lord God to send your majesty long life and good health, to God's glory, your own honor, and the wealth of this noble realm.

From Richmond, the 11th day of July, the 32nd year of your majesty's most noble reign. Your majesty's most humble sister and servant, Anne, the daughter of Cleves.

Anne of Cleves